To

Michelle

From

Grandma and Grandpa

Date

November 2001

With all our love!

Visit Christian Art Gifts, Inc. at www.christianartgifts.com.

A Light for My Path

Published by Christian Art Gifts, Inc.

Previously published as
TouchPoints Bible Promises
First printing by Tyndale House Publishers in 2000.

Scripture selection and note writing primarily by Douglas J. Rumford
General editors: Ronald A. Beers and V. Gilbert Beers
Contributing writers: Douglas J. Rumford, Rhonda K. O'Brien, V. Gilbert Beers,
Ronald A. Beers, Shawn A. Harrison, Jonathan Gray, and Brian R. Coffey.

Designed by Christian Art Gifts
Cover and interior images used under license from Shutterstock.com

Printed in China

ISBN 978-1-4321-3260-6

20 21 22 23 24 25 26 27 28 29 – 10 9 8 7 6 5 4 3 2 1

A LIGHT FOR MY PATH

Christian art gifts®

Your word
is a *lamp*
for my feet
and a *light*
for my path.

Psalm 119:105

PREFACE

Your decrees are my treasure; they are truly my heart's delight ... I rejoice in your word like one who finds great treasure. PSALM 119:111, 162

Your laws remain true today; for everything serves your plans ... All your words are true; all your just laws will stand forever. PSALM 119:91, 160

What a treasure we have in God's word! The Holy Bible is relevant to today's issues and gives solid guidance for daily living.

In this book you will find close to one hundred topics for daily living and what the Bible says about each one. Each topic is listed alphabetically and is accompanied by questions, Scripture passages, and comments. In the index at the back of this book, you will find a complete listing of all the topics for quick reference. You can read through this book page by page or use it as a reference guide for topics of particular interest to you.

While we could not cover all topics, questions, and Scriptures related to the subject of this book, our prayer is that you will continue to deliberately search God's word. May you find God's answers as he longs to be your daily guide. Enjoy your treasure hunt!

The Editors

ABANDONMENT

Will God abandon me during my hard times?

Even if my father and mother abandon me, the LORD will hold me close. *PSALM 27:10*

Even if those on whom we most rely desert or neglect us, God never will. In fact, our difficulties can become the means to experience God's presence even more intimately.

Does God promise to be with me at some times, but not at others?

Jesus came and told his disciples, … "Be sure of this: I am with you always, even to the end of the age." *MATTHEW 28:18, 20*

I will ask the Father, and he will give you another Counselor, who will never leave you. *JOHN 14:16*

We are hunted down, but God never abandons us. We get knocked down, but we get up again and keep going. *2 CORINTHIANS 4:9*

Stay away from the love of money; be satisfied with what you have. For God has said, "I will never fail you. I will never forsake you." *HEBREWS 13:5*

God will

generously

PROVIDE

all you need.

2 Corinthians 9:8

ABUNDANCE

Under what circumstances does God promise abundance to us?

This same God who takes care of me will supply all your needs from his glorious riches, which have been given to us in Christ Jesus. *PHILIPPIANS 4:19*

God's abundant provision is a gracious gift. When we give what God requires we receive more than we could ever desire.

The LORD your God will make you successful in everything you do. He will give you many children and numerous livestock, and your fields will produce abundant harvests, for the LORD will delight in being good to you as he was to your ancestors. *DEUTERONOMY 30:9*

God is not stingy and resentful in supplying our needs. He loves to lavish his abundance on those with grateful hearts.

Why does God give us abundant gifts?

God will generously provide all you need. Then you will always have everything you need and plenty left over to share with others. *2 CORINTHIANS 9:8*

God wants us to have everything we need. But we don't get to keep what we receive; we get to give it away. God is looking for us to share his abundance with others.

ACCEPTANCE

How can I know that God accepts me?

There is only one God, and there is only one way of being accepted by him. He makes people right with himself only by faith, whether they are Jews or Gentiles. ROMANS 3:30

If we say we have no sin, we are only fooling ourselves and refusing to accept the truth. But if we confess our sins to him, he is faithful and just to forgive us and to cleanse us from every wrong. If we claim we have not sinned, we are calling God a liar and showing that his word has no place in our hearts. 1 JOHN 1:8-10

God's acceptance is not based on what we do, but on faith in Jesus Christ.

How can my faith help me accept circumstances I cannot change?

It is a good thing to receive wealth from God and the good health to enjoy it. To enjoy your work and accept your lot in life—that is indeed a gift from God. ECCLESIASTES 5:19

You must accept whatever situation the Lord has put you in, and continue on as you were when God first called you. This is my rule for all the churches. 1 CORINTHIANS 7:17

ADDICTION

How can God break the power of addiction in my life?

When the Holy Spirit controls our lives, he will produce this kind of fruit in us: love, joy, peace, patience, kindness, goodness, faithfulness, gentleness, and self-control. Here there is no conflict with the law. *GALATIANS 5:22-23*

Don't copy the behavior and customs of this world, but let God transform you into a new person by changing the way you think. Then you will know what God wants you to do, and you will know how good and pleasing and perfect his will really is. *ROMANS 12:2*

Every child of God defeats this evil world by trusting Christ to give the victory. And the ones who win this battle against the world are the ones who believe that Jesus is the Son of God. *1 JOHN 5:4-5*

How do I ask God to help me be free of an addiction?

Humble yourselves under the mighty power of God, and in his good time he will honor you. Give all your worries and cares to God, for he cares about what happens to you. *1 PETER 5:6-7*

AGING

Will God continue to be with me as I age?

I will be your God throughout your lifetime—until your hair is white with age. I made you, and I will care for you. I will carry you along and save you. *ISAIAH 46:4*

God's love lasts for all our days. This promise gives us a wonderful picture of God's care. He walks alongside us and carries us when we can no longer walk.

Will I still be useful in my old age?

Even in old age they will still produce fruit; they will remain vital and green. *PSALM 92:14*

Regardless of our age, we can be productive and vital, telling others of God's goodness.

What can lead to a longer life?

My child, never forget the things I have taught you. Store my commands in your heart, for they will give you a long and satisfying life. *PROVERBS 3:1-2*

Fear of the Lord, which involves knowing and obeying the Lord and his commands, leads to a satisfying life and often a long life as well. Is it surprising that a close relationship with the author of life helps us enrich and lengthen our lives?

The unfailing *love*
of the LORD never ends!
By his *mercies* we have
been kept from
complete destruction.
Great is his faithfulness;
his *mercies* begin
afresh each day.

Lamentations 3:22-23

ANGER

Is God angry with me?

God is my shield, saving those whose hearts are true and right. God is a judge who is perfectly fair. He is angry with the wicked every day. PSALM 7:10-11

To the pure you show yourself pure, but to the wicked you show yourself hostile. You rescue those who are humble, but you humiliate the proud. PSALM 18:26-27

God cannot tolerate sin and rebellion against him. But he is ready to forgive, because he is kind and merciful. Those who humbly confess their sin and turn to him in faith receive God's abundant love and mercy instead of anger.

The LORD is kind and merciful, slow to get angry, full of unfailing love. PSALM 145:8

What can I do to reduce my angry responses?

A gentle answer turns away wrath, but harsh words stir up anger. PROVERBS 15:1

People with good sense restrain their anger; they earn esteem by overlooking wrongs. PROVERBS 19:11

Don't sin by letting anger gain control over you. Think about it overnight and remain silent. PSALM 4:4

ASSURANCE

How can I be assured of God's lasting care for me?

The unfailing love of the Lord never ends! By his mercies we have been kept from complete destruction. Great is his faithfulness; his mercies begin afresh each day.
LAMENTATIONS 3:22-23

Can anything ever separate us from Christ's love? Does it mean he no longer loves us if we have trouble or calamity, or are persecuted, or are hungry or cold or in danger or threatened with death? … I am convinced that nothing can ever separate us from his love. Death can't, and life can't. The angels can't, and the demons can't. Our fears for today, our worries about tomorrow, and even the powers of hell can't keep God's love away. Whether we are high above the sky or in the deepest ocean, nothing in all creation will ever be able to separate us from the love of God that is revealed in Christ Jesus our Lord. *ROMANS 8:35, 38-39*

The assurance of God's love gives us courage to come to him with any problem, struggle, or concern. Our prayers are never interruptions to the Lord. When we knock, the door is always open to us.

BACKSLIDING

What do I do when I've fallen away from God?

All have sinned; all fall short of God's glorious standard. Yet now God in his gracious kindness declares us not guilty. He has done this through Christ Jesus, who has freed us by taking away our sins. *ROMANS 3:23-24*

Because of our sinful nature, we might fall away from God. Yet once we've identified and confessed our sin, God is faithful to forgive us. There is no sin so great we cannot come back to God.

How can I avoid backsliding?

Obey God because you are his children. Don't slip back into your old ways of doing evil; you didn't know any better then. *1 PETER 1:14*

Keep alert and pray. Otherwise temptation will overpower you. For though the spirit is willing enough, the body is weak! *MATTHEW 26:41*

Remember that the temptations that come into your life are no different from what others experience. And God is faithful. He will keep the temptation from becoming so strong that you can't stand up against it. When you are tempted, he will show you a way out so that you will not give in to it. *1 CORINTHIANS 10:13*

BEGINNINGS

How do we get a new start?

Those who become Christians become new persons. They are not the same anymore, for the old life is gone. A new life has begun! 2 CORINTHIANS 5:17

Those who believe in Jesus Christ are not simply turning over a new leaf; they are re-created as people! They have a new life.

How many opportunities does God give me to begin anew?

Great is his faithfulness; his mercies begin afresh each day. LAMENTATIONS 3:23

We don't have to wait for New Year's resolutions to start over again. God renews his mercies to us every single day. We don't have to be burdened by yesterday's failures or regrets.

How can I know God is with me as I begin a new work?

I am sure that God, who began the good work within you, will continue his work until it is finally finished on that day when Christ Jesus comes back again. PHILIPPIANS 1:6

God has begun not only the work of salvation in us, but also the work of transforming every aspect of our lives. We invite him to work in our relationships, our work, our recreation, and every other part of our lives.

BELONGING

What happens to those who belong to God?

We have this assurance: Those who belong to God will live; their bodies will rise again! Those who sleep in the earth will rise up and sing for joy! For God's light of life will fall like dew on his people in the place of the dead! *ISAIAH 26:19*

Belonging to God is an eternal relationship, not merely for this world, but for the world to come. The grave is not the last chapter, merely the transitional one.

No one wants to be alone. How can I know I belong in fellowship with God's people?

Just as our bodies have many parts and each part has a special function, so it is with Christ's body. We are all parts of his one body, and each of us has different work to do. And since we are all one body in Christ, we belong to each other, and each of us needs all the others. *ROMANS 12:4-5*

Belonging to God makes you part of Christ's body, the church. You belong in fellowship with God's people because you are in fellowship with God.

BETRAYAL

How do I handle betrayal - when someone hasn't been faithful to me?

As for this friend of mine, he betrayed me; he broke his promises. His words are as smooth as cream, but in his heart is war. His words are as soothing as lotion, but underneath are daggers! Give your burdens to the LORD, and he will take care of you. He will not permit the godly to slip and fall.

PSALM 55:20-22

When others are unfaithful to us, we can take great comfort in God's unwavering faithfulness. We anchor our faith in the Lord, not in other frail human beings.

Where do we find the courage and strength to forgive our betrayer?

Forgive us our sins, just as we have forgiven those who have sinned against us. And don't let us yield to temptation, but deliver us from the evil one. If you forgive those who sin against you, your heavenly Father will forgive you.

MATTHEW 6:12-14

Forgiveness is the only road to freedom. A forgiven person forgives. Nothing that anyone has done against us compares with what we have done against God. Refusing to forgive another means we don't realize just how much God has forgiven us.

BIBLE

What is promised to us when we study the Bible?

Your words are what sustain me. They bring me great joy and are my heart's delight, for I bear your name, O LORD God Almighty. *JEREMIAH 15:16*

The Bible sustains and directs us physically, mentally, emotionally, and spiritually, bringing lasting joy and deep satisfaction in life.

You will know the truth, and the truth will set you free. *JOHN 8:32*

Reading the Bible tells us how to be set free from sin.

How can a young person stay pure? By obeying your word and following its rules. *PSALM 119:9*

Your decrees please me; they give me wise advice. *PSALM 119:24*

I am but a foreigner here on earth; I need the guidance of your commands. Don't hide them from me! *PSALM 119:19*

Your word is a lamp for my feet and a light for my path. *PSALM 119:105*

Reading the Bible guides us in daily living, giving us the best counsel for our problems.

Your promise revives me; it comforts me in all my troubles. *PSALM 119:50*

Reading the Bible gives us hope for the future.

You will know
the *truth*, and
THE TRUTH
will set you free.

John 8:32

BLESSINGS

How has God promised to bless his people?

Blessed are those who trust in the LORD and have made the LORD their hope and confidence. *JEREMIAH 17:7*

The only thing I didn't do, which I do in the other churches, was to become a burden to you. Please forgive me for this wrong! *2 CORINTHIANS 12:13*

Jesus Christ blesses us with forgiveness and redemption. God the Father blesses us with the assurance that we are loved and of infinite worth. The Holy Spirit blesses us with fellowship and the continual presence of God.

The LORD God is our light and protector. He gives us grace and glory. No good thing will the LORD withhold from those who do what is right. *PSALM 84:11*

God promises to bless those who do what is right; he doesn't extend the same promise to those who don't do what is right.

If you help the poor, you are lending to the LORD—and he will repay you! *PROVERBS 19:17*

How does the promise of blessing affect us when we are weary or discouraged?

Don't get tired of doing what is good. Don't get discouraged and give up, for we will reap a harvest of blessing at the appropriate time. *GALATIANS 6:9*

BURNOUT

Is something wrong with me if I am burning out?

He gives power to those who are tired and worn out;
he offers strength to the weak. Even youths will become
exhausted, and young men will give up. But those who wait
on the LORD will find new strength. They will fly high on
wings like eagles. They will run and not grow weary. They will
walk and not faint. *ISAIAH 40:29-31*

How can I find new joy and energy?

The Sovereign LORD, the Holy One of Israel, says, "Only in
returning to me and waiting for me will you be saved. In
quietness and confidence is your strength." *ISAIAH 30:15*

*Burnout comes when we lose our connection to the Lord. When we live
out of our love for him, we experience his strength working through us.*

Jesus said, "Come to me, all of you who are weary and carry
heavy burdens, and I will give you rest. Take my yoke upon
you. Let me teach you, because I am humble and gentle, and
you will find rest for your souls." *MATTHEW 11:28-29*

*Burnout often comes when we take too much responsibility
on ourselves. When we put our confidence in the Lord, the
burden lightens.*

BUSYNESS

Does God expect me to be busy all the time?

He lets me rest in green meadows; he leads me beside peaceful streams. *PSALM 23:2*

Jesus said, "Come to me, all of you who are weary and carry heavy burdens, and I will give you rest. Take my yoke upon you. Let me teach you, because I am humble and gentle, and you will find rest for your souls." *MATTHEW 11:28-29*

Activity itself is not a virtue; it can actually be a detriment to our spiritual lives. The Lord invites us to rest and be refreshed in his care.

What is the antidote to empty busyness?

Teach us to make the most of our time, so that we may grow in wisdom. *PSALM 90:12*

Be careful how you live, not as fools but as those who are wise. Make the most of every opportunity for doing good in these evil days. Don't act thoughtlessly, but try to understand what the Lord wants you to do. Don't be drunk with wine, because that will ruin your life. Instead, let the Holy Spirit fill and control you. Then you will sing psalms and hymns and spiritual songs among yourselves, making music to the Lord in your hearts. And you will always give thanks for everything to God the Father in the name of our Lord Jesus Christ. *EPHESIANS 5:15-20*

CALL OF GOD

Is God calling me to serve him?

There are different kinds of spiritual gifts, but it is the same Holy Spirit who is the source of them all. There are different kinds of service in the church, but it is the same Lord we are serving. There are different ways God works in our lives, but it is the same God who does the work through all of us. A spiritual gift is given to each of us as a means of helping the entire church. *1 CORINTHIANS 12:4-7*

God's call is based on his promise of the Holy Spirit at work in our lives. Each of us is called to serve the Lord with the gifts we have been given.

What does God provide so I can fulfill his call?

Now, may the God of peace, who brought again from the dead our Lord Jesus, equip you with all you need for doing his will. May he produce in you, through the power of Jesus Christ, all that is pleasing to him. Jesus is the great Shepherd of the sheep by an everlasting covenant, signed with his blood. To him be glory forever and ever. Amen. *HEBREWS 13:20-21*

Where God calls, he equips. The power of the resurrected Lord ensures that we fulfill God's call in our lives.

CHALLENGES

Why does God allow challenges in our lives?

Dear brothers and sisters, whenever trouble comes your way, let it be an opportunity for joy. For when your faith is tested, your endurance has a chance to grow. So let it grow, for when your endurance is fully developed, you will be strong in character and ready for anything. *JAMES 1:2-4*

What has God given me to help me face my challenges?

Be strong and very courageous. Obey all the laws Moses gave you. Do not turn away from them, and you will be successful in everything you do. *JOSHUA 1:7*

God has given us his word to direct us. The promise of success is embedded in our commitment to obedience.

David continued, "Be strong and courageous, and do the work. Don't be afraid or discouraged by the size of the task, for the LORD God, my God, is with you. He will not fail you or forsake you. He will see to it that all the work related to the Temple of the LORD is finished correctly." *1 CHRONICLES 28:20*

Instead of being discouraged by the size of the task, we should be encouraged by the limitless power of God.

Be strong
and *very*
courageous.

Joshua 1:7

CHANGE

Where can I find security and hope in the midst of tumult and change?

LORD, you remain the same forever! Your throne continues from generation to generation. *LAMENTATIONS 5:19*

Whatever is good and perfect comes to us from God above, who created all heaven's lights. Unlike them, he never changes or casts shifting shadows. *JAMES 1:17*

Jesus Christ is the same yesterday, today, and forever. *HEBREWS 13:8*

The grass withers, and the flowers fade, but the word of our God stands forever. *MARK 13:31*

How can I hope that I can change for the better?

Those who become Christians become new persons. They are not the same anymore, for the old life is gone. A new life has begun! *2 CORINTHIANS 5:17*

I am sure that God, who began the good work within you, will continue his work until it is finally finished on that day when Christ Jesus comes back again. *PHILIPPIANS 1:6*

A great work takes a long time to complete. Though we are converted in a moment of faith, the process of transformation into Christlikeness takes a lifetime. While it may appear slow to us, it's relentless and certain.

CHARACTER

Will God do anything to change my character, or is it all up to me?

When the Holy Spirit controls our lives, he will produce this kind of fruit in us: love, joy, peace, patience, kindness, goodness, faithfulness, gentleness, and self-control. Here there is no conflict with the law. GALATIANS 5:22-23

A transformed character reflects God's work within us and our own choices. The Holy Spirit awakens our desire for love, integrity, and responsibility, but we must choose these in every situation.

What does God promise as we mature in godly character?

We can rejoice, too, when we run into problems and trials, for we know that they are good for us—they help us learn to endure. And endurance develops strength of character in us, and character strengthens our confident expectation of salvation. And this expectation will not disappoint us. For we know how dearly God loves us, because he has given us the Holy Spirit to fill our hearts with his love. ROMANS 5:3-5

As we mature in our faith, we will become stronger and stronger people. Character is like a muscle—it gets stronger with exercise. As our character develops, our confidence in our salvation increases, and the assurance of God's love fills our hearts.

CHRISTLIKENESS

How can I ever expect to be like Jesus?

All of us have had that veil removed so that we can be mirrors that brightly reflect the glory of the Lord. And as the Spirit of the Lord works within us, we become more and more like him and reflect his glory even more. *2 CORINTHIANS 3:18*

When we trust in Christ for salvation, he begins to work in our hearts. As the Spirit works within us, he changes us to be more and more like Jesus.

I myself no longer live, but Christ lives in me. So I live my life in this earthly body by trusting in the Son of God, who loved me and gave himself for me. *GALATIANS 2:20*

The truth is, anyone who believes in me will do the same works I have done, and even greater works, because I am going to be with the Father. You can ask for anything in my name, and I will do it, because the work of the Son brings glory to the Father. Yes, ask anything in my name, and I will do it! *JOHN 14:12-14*

We should not simply ask for things from the Lord; we should ask to be like the Lord. We have the amazing promise that we can become like him and do what he has done!

CHURCH

Do we really need the church?

I pray that you will begin to understand the incredible greatness of his power for us who believe him. This is the same mighty power that raised Christ from the dead and seated him in the place of honor at God's right hand in the heavenly realms. Now he is far above any ruler or authority or power or leader or anything else in this world or in the world to come. And God has put all things under the authority of Christ, and he gave him this authority for the benefit of the church. And the church is his body; it is filled by Christ, who fills everything everywhere with his presence. *EPHESIANS 1:19-23*

God wants to do great things in the church. The people of God are equipped with the resurrection power of Jesus Christ and are the emissaries of the Lord who rules over all! When we come together with this vision, we have confidence that God will do more than we could have ever imagined.

But sometimes the church seems so weak. How can we have hope for the church?

Upon this rock I will build my church, and all the powers of hell will not conquer it. *MATTHEW 16:18*

COMFORT

How does God comfort us?

Even when I walk through the dark valley of death, I will not be afraid, for you are close beside me. Your rod and your staff protect and comfort me. *PSALM 23:4*

God blesses those who mourn, for they will be comforted. *MATTHEW 5:4*

God comforts us by staying close beside us in difficulty, by blessing us even when we are in mourning, and by promising us joy to come.

The LORD is close to the brokenhearted; he rescues those who are crushed in spirit. *PSALM 34:18*

The LORD helps the fallen and lifts up those bent beneath their loads. *PSALM 145:14*

I have told you all this so that you may have peace in me. Here on earth you will have many trials and sorrows. But take heart, because I have overcome the world. *JOHN 16:33*

He will feed his flock like a shepherd. He will carry the lambs in his arms, holding them close to his heart. He will gently lead the mother sheep with their young. *ISAIAH 40:11*

When we are overwhelmed, God comforts us with his presence. He calms our hearts, renews our confidence, and awakens our hope.

The LORD is *close* to the brokenhearted; he *rescues* those who are crushed in spirit.

Psalm 34:18

CONFIDENCE

Where do we find confidence for every day?

The LORD is my light and my salvation—so why should I be afraid? The LORD protects me from danger—so why should I tremble? *PSALM 27:1*

The LORD keeps watch over you as you come and go, both now and forever. *PSALM 121:8*

How can we have confidence in the face of life's greatest hardships?

Trust in the LORD with all your heart; do not depend on your own understanding. Seek his will in all you do, and he will direct your paths. *PROVERBS 3:5-6*

Not that I was ever in need, for I have learned how to get along happily whether I have much or little. I know how to live on almost nothing or with everything. I have learned the secret of living in every situation, whether it is with a full stomach or empty, with plenty or little. For I can do everything with the help of Christ who gives me the strength I need. *PHILIPPIANS 4:11-13*

Our happiness rises and falls, but our steady confidence comes from the consistency of Christ. We depend on Christ—not on circumstances.

CONFLICT

Shouldn't those who believe in Jesus Christ be free from conflict?

The LORD is my light and my salvation—so why should I be afraid? The LORD protects me from danger—so why should I tremble? When evil people come to destroy me, when my enemies and foes attack me, they will stumble and fall. Though a mighty army surrounds me, my heart will know no fear. Even if they attack me, I remain confident. *PSALM 27:1-3*

He rescues me and keeps me safe from the battle waged against me, even though many still oppose me. *PSALM 55:18*

While God doesn't keep us out of all conflict, he is present with us in it.

How can I find strength to respond to conflict in God's way?

Dear friends, never avenge yourselves. Leave that to God. For it is written, "I will take vengeance; I will repay those who deserve it," says the Lord. Instead, do what the Scriptures say: "If your enemies are hungry, feed them. If they are thirsty, give them something to drink, and they will be ashamed of what they have done to you." Don't let evil get the best of you, but conquer evil by doing good. *ROMANS 12:19-21*

Peace lies in the power of love, not the love of power. If we trust in God, he promises to protect and vindicate us.

CONTENTMENT

How can I experience contentment?

True religion with contentment is great wealth. After all, we didn't bring anything with us when we came into the world, and we certainly cannot carry anything with us when we die. *1 TIMOTHY 6:6-7*

You will keep in perfect peace all who trust in you, whose thoughts are fixed on you! *ISAIAH 26:3*

As we know Jesus better, his divine power gives us everything we need for living a godly life. He has called us to receive his own glory and goodness! *2 PETER 1:3*

When we have Jesus Christ, we have all we need. He teaches us to discern the valuable things in life from the distractions. Contentment comes from being in Christ's presence, not from accumulating worldly possessions.

How can we find freedom from the sins of comparison, competition, and jealousy that disturb our contentment?

The LORD is my shepherd; I have everything I need. He lets me rest in green meadows; he leads me beside peaceful streams. He renews my strength. He guides me along right paths, bringing honor to his name. *PSALM 23:1-3*

COURAGE

Where do I turn when I'm afraid?

The LORD is my light and my salvation—so why should I be afraid? The LORD protects me from danger—so why should I tremble? *PSALM 27:1*

Don't be afraid, for I am with you. Do not be dismayed, for I am your God. I will strengthen you. I will help you. I will uphold you with my victorious right hand. *ISAIAH 41:10*

Will God take away the things that frighten me?

All the believers were united as they lifted their voices in prayer: … "O Lord, hear their threats, and give your servants great boldness in their preaching. Send your healing power; may miraculous signs and wonders be done through the name of your holy servant Jesus." After this prayer, the building where they were meeting shook, and they were all filled with the Holy Spirit. And they preached God's message with boldness. *ACTS 4:24, 29-31*

Courage comes from the Holy Spirit. The early church was constantly threatened by the religious leaders in Jerusalem. They did not pray for the threats to end but for the courage to face those threats. The Holy Spirit gives us the boldness to turn threats into opportunities for testifying to our faith.

CRISIS

Shouldn't those who believe in God be free from crisis?

I have told you all this so that you may have peace in me. Here on earth you will have many trials and sorrows. But take heart, because I have overcome the world. *JOHN 16:33*

Crisis should not surprise us. We expect crisis and difficulty because we live in a fallen world. Jesus' warning keeps us from panic, and his promise of victory keeps us from discouragement.

Trust me in your times of trouble, and I will rescue you, and you will give me glory. *PSALM 50:15*

What happens to us through times of crisis?

We can rejoice, too, when we run into problems and trials, for we know that they are good for us—they help us learn to endure. And endurance develops strength of character in us, and character strengthens our confident expectation of salvation. *ROMANS 5:3-4*

Since I know it is all for Christ's good, I am quite content with my weaknesses and with insults, hardships, persecutions, and calamities. For when I am weak, then I am strong. *2 CORINTHIANS 12:10*

Spiritual strength can grow from physical weakness. Being physically weak teaches us that we cannot rely on our own strength to see us through—we need God's strength.

Trust me in your times of trouble, and I will *rescue* you, and you will give me glory.

Psalm 50:15

DEATH

Is death the end of all hope?

There are many rooms in my Father's home, and I am going to prepare a place for you. If this were not so, I would tell you plainly. *JOHN 14:2*

Jesus told her, "I am the resurrection and the life. Those who believe in me, even though they die like everyone else, will live again." *JOHN 11:25*

Physical death is not the end, it is but a stage in life. Physical death is the door to eternal life for those who believe in Jesus Christ. Those who believe are promised a glorious future—the resurrection of the body and everlasting life.

What is the hope for those who trust Jesus Christ as Savior?

If you confess with your mouth that Jesus is Lord and believe in your heart that God raised him from the dead, you will be saved. For it is by believing in your heart that you are made right with God, and it is by confessing with your mouth that you are saved. *ROMANS 10:9-10*

Since Christ lives within you, even though your body will die because of sin, your spirit is alive because you have been made right with God. *ROMANS 8:10*

We have hope because Jesus Christ defeated death!

DECISIONS

What do we do when we do not know what to do?

Trust in the LORD with all your heart; do not depend on your own understanding. Seek his will in all you do, and he will direct your paths. Don't be impressed with your own wisdom. Instead, fear the LORD and turn your back on evil.

PROVERBS 3:5-7

Trust the Lord to direct your steps, even when the way is confusing. God will guide you.

What kind of help does God give us?

If you need wisdom—if you want to know what God wants you to do—ask him, and he will gladly tell you. He will not resent your asking. But when you ask him, be sure that you really expect him to answer, for a doubtful mind is as unsettled as a wave of the sea that is driven and tossed by the wind. People like that should not expect to receive anything from the Lord. They can't make up their minds. They waver back and forth in everything they do. JAMES 1:5-8

Some people fear that they are bothering God with their problems. Nothing could be further from the truth. God is looking for ways to help us because he loves us. Our commitment to him releases his resources for us.

DEPRESSION

What can I do when I'm depressed?

Even though the fig trees have no blossoms, and there are no grapes on the vine; even though the olive crop fails, and the fields lie empty and barren; even though the flocks die in the fields, and the cattle barns are empty, yet I will rejoice in the LORD! I will be joyful in the God of my salvation. The Sovereign LORD is my strength! He will make me as surefooted as a deer and bring me safely over the mountains.
HABAKKUK 3:17-19

Much depression is caused by trusting in the things of this world instead of in God. We will be disappointed if our happiness is based on security, prestige, possessions, and popularity. These things come and go. Trusting in God helps us travel through the toughest times with surefooted confidence.

Where can I find inspiration and encouragement in times of depression?

Those who listen to instruction will prosper; those who trust the LORD will be happy. *PROVERBS 16:20*

Jesus said, "Come to me, all of you who are weary and carry heavy burdens, and I will give you rest." *MATTHEW 11:28*

DISCERNMENT

When I am confused, where do I turn for clarity, wisdom, understanding, and direction?

If you need wisdom—if you want to know what God wants you to do—ask him, and he will gladly tell you. He will not resent your asking. But when you ask him, be sure that you really expect him to answer, for a doubtful mind is as unsettled as a wave of the sea that is driven and tossed by the wind. People like that should not expect to receive anything from the Lord. They can't make up their minds. They waver back and forth in everything they do. JAMES 1:5-8

What are the benefits of discernment?

Happy is the person who finds wisdom and gains understanding. PROVERBS 3:13

My child, don't lose sight of good planning and insight. Hang on to them, for they fill you with life and bring you honor and respect. They keep you safe on your way and keep your feet from stumbling. PROVERBS 3:21-23

If you live a life guided by wisdom, you won't limp or stumble as you run. PROVERBS 4:12

Wisdom will multiply your days and add years to your life. PROVERBS 9:11

DOUBT

How can I trust God when I can't see a way out of my problem?

Nothing is impossible with God. *LUKE 1:37*

Doubt often arises because we look at the problem instead of looking up to God. God is not limited by our circumstances or by our lack of resources or abilities. Sarah and Abraham, Mary and Joseph, and many other of God's people across the centuries have learned that God can do anything.

Jesus told them, "I assure you, if you have faith and don't doubt, you can do things like this and much more. You can even say to this mountain, 'May God lift you up and throw you into the sea,' and it will happen. If you believe, you will receive whatever you ask for in prayer." *MATTHEW 21:21-22*

The Spirit is God's guarantee that he will give us everything he promised and that he has purchased us to be his own people. This is just one more reason for us to praise our glorious God. *EPHESIANS 1:14*

God has said, "I will never fail you. I will never forsake you." *HEBREWS 13:5*

Faith comes from listening to this message of good news— the Good News about Christ. *ROMANS 10:17*

God has said,
"I will never fail
you. I will never
forsake you."

Hebrews 13:5

ENCOURAGEMENT

What do I do when I feel overwhelmed?

We also pray that you will be strengthened with his glorious power so that you will have all the patience and endurance you need. May you be filled with joy, always thanking the Father, who has enabled you to share the inheritance that belongs to God's holy people, who live in the light. For he has rescued us from the one who rules in the kingdom of darkness, and he has brought us into the Kingdom of his dear Son. God has purchased our freedom with his blood and has forgiven all our sins. COLOSSIANS 1:11-14

Our encouragement comes from what God has done for us. He has given us the power to be patient and persistent and to keep our minds set on the great hope that awaits us. When we remember that we are already free, the problems of this world lose much of their power over us.

What good can my struggles produce?

In his kindness God called you to his eternal glory by means of Jesus Christ. After you have suffered a little while, he will restore, support, and strengthen you, and he will place you on a firm foundation. All power is his forever and ever. Amen. 1 PETER 5:10-11

ENDURANCE

Where do I find the strength to keep going when I'm tempted to give up?

Don't get tired of doing what is good. Don't get discouraged and give up, for we will reap a harvest of blessing at the appropriate time. *GALATIANS 6:9*

I am sure that God, who began the good work within you, will continue his work until it is finally finished on that day when Christ Jesus comes back again. *PHILIPPIANS 1:6*

If I already believe in Christ, why do I have to endure?

Be very glad—because these trials will make you partners with Christ in his suffering, and afterward you will have the wonderful joy of sharing his glory when it is displayed to all the world. *1 PETER 4:13*

If we are faithful to the end, trusting God just as firmly as when we first believed, we will share in all that belongs to Christ. *HEBREWS 3:14*

Those who endure to the end will be saved. *MATTHEW 24:13*

Endurance is an essential quality of Jesus' followers. Though we have the promise of eternal life, we also face the prospect of living in a fallen world out to compromise and destroy our faith. God promises that those who endure will not only survive, but reign with Christ!

ENERGY

Why do I sometimes find myself weary and tired?

Have you never heard or understood? Don't you know that the LORD is the everlasting God, the Creator of all the earth? He never grows faint or weary. No one can measure the depths of his understanding. He gives power to those who are tired and worn out; he offers strength to the weak. Even youths will become exhausted, and young men will give up. But those who wait on the LORD will find new strength. They will fly high on wings like eagles. They will run and not grow weary. They will walk and not faint. ISAIAH 40:28-31

As human beings, we have limitations. We get hungry, tired, and hurt. We are not self-sufficient. Instead of relying on ourselves, we need to rely on the Lord. Like the eagle that soars on the currents of wind, we can trust the Lord to carry us onward.

What has God given me as a source of continual energy?

I pray that from his glorious, unlimited resources he will give you mighty inner strength through his Holy Spirit.
EPHESIANS 3:16

The Sovereign LORD is my strength! He will make me as surefooted as a deer and bring me safely over the mountains.
HABAKKUK 3:19

EVIL

How do I confront evil?

The Devil took him to Jerusalem, to the highest point of the Temple, and said, "If you are the Son of God, jump off! For the Scriptures say, 'He orders his angels to protect you. And they will hold you with their hands to keep you from striking your foot on a stone.'" Jesus responded, "The Scriptures also say, 'Do not test the Lord your God.'" *MATTHEW 4:5-7*

Humble yourselves before God. Resist the Devil, and he will flee from you. *JAMES 4:7*

The devil has less power than we think. The devil can tempt us, but he cannot coerce us. He could take Jesus to the top of the temple, but he could not push him off. He can dangle the bait in front of us, but he cannot put the hook in our mouth. We can resist the devil as Jesus did—by responding to the lies of temptation with the truth of God's word.

You belong to God, my dear children. You have already won your fight with these false prophets, because the Spirit who lives in you is greater than the spirit who lives in the world. *1 JOHN 4:4*

We must never forget that the Holy Spirit is great enough to overcome any threat against us.

FAILURE

What is failure in God's eyes?

Work hard and cheerfully at whatever you do, as though you were working for the Lord rather than for people. Remember that the Lord will give you an inheritance as your reward, and the Master you are serving is Christ. COLOSSIANS 3:23-24

Often our sense of failure is determined by the level of approval from others. Scripture reminds us to define success in terms of faithfulness to God. God will reward our faithfulness even if we fail in the eyes of the world.

What do I do when I have failed the Lord?

If your people Israel are defeated by their enemies because they have sinned against you, and if they turn to you and call on your name and pray to you here in this Temple, then hear from heaven and forgive their sins and return them to this land you gave their ancestors. 1 KINGS 8:33-34

Turning to God in repentance and trust is the best response we can have to failure.

Great is his faithfulness; his mercies begin afresh each day.
LAMENTATIONS 3:23

Every day is a new start in God's mercy. By God's grace and love we are freed from the burden of sin and failure so that we can start afresh.

Work hard and *cheerfully* at whatever you do, as though you were working for the Lord rather than for people.

Colossians 3:23

FAITH

What does faith mean for my everyday life?

Now God in his gracious kindness declares us not guilty. He has done this through Christ Jesus, who has freed us by taking away our sins. For God sent Jesus to take the punishment for our sins and to satisfy God's anger against us. We are made right with God when we believe that Jesus shed his blood, sacrificing his life for us. God was being entirely fair and just when he did not punish those who sinned in former times. *ROMANS 3:24-25*

You will keep in perfect peace all who trust in you, whose thoughts are fixed on you! *ISAIAH 26:3*

How much faith must I have?

"You didn't have enough faith," Jesus told them. "I assure you, even if you had faith as small as a mustard seed you could say to this mountain, 'Move from here to there,' and it would move. Nothing would be impossible." *MATTHEW 17:20*

The mustard seed was often used to illustrate the smallest seed known to man. Jesus says that faith is not a matter of size or quantity. We do not have to have great faith in God; we have to have faith in a great God.

FAITHFULNESS

How is God faithful to me?

The LORD your God is indeed God. He is the faithful God who keeps his covenant for a thousand generations and constantly loves those who love him and obey his commands. *DEUTERONOMY 7:9*

The love of the LORD remains forever with those who fear him. His salvation extends to the children's children of those who are faithful to his covenant, of those who obey his commandments! *PSALM 103:17-18*

Why should I be faithful?

Oh, the joys of those who do not follow the advice of the wicked, or stand around with sinners, or join in with scoffers. But they delight in doing everything the LORD wants; day and night they think about his law. They are like trees planted along the riverbank, bearing fruit each season without fail. Their leaves never wither, and in all they do, they prosper. *PSALM 1:1-3*

The quality of our character affects the quality of our life. Integrity brings continual vitality and bears lasting fruit.

If we are faithful to the end, trusting God just as firmly as when we first believed, we will share in all that belongs to Christ. *HEBREWS 3:14*

FAMILY

How can I best care for my family?

Children, obey your parents because you belong to the Lord, for this is the right thing to do. "Honor your father and mother." This is the first of the Ten Commandments that ends with a promise. And this is the promise: If you honor your father and mother, "you will live a long life, full of blessing." And now a word to you fathers. Don't make your children angry by the way you treat them. Rather, bring them up with the discipline and instruction approved by the Lord.

EPHESIANS 6:1-4

Honoring our families is one of the pathways to receiving God's promises. Parents are entrusted to teach their children to walk in God's ways and to discipline in love. Children are to respond with respect and obedience. When these happen, good things follow.

What will God do for my family?

Praise the LORD! Happy are those who fear the LORD. Yes, happy are those who delight in doing what he commands. Their children will be successful everywhere; an entire generation of godly people will be blessed. They themselves will be wealthy, and their good deeds will never be forgotten.

PSALM 112:1-3

FEAR

What can I do when I am overcome with fear?

God is our refuge and strength, always ready to help in times of trouble. So we will not fear, even if earthquakes come and the mountains crumble into the sea. *PSALM 46:1-2*

God has not given us a spirit of fear and timidity, but of power, love, and self-discipline. *2 TIMOTHY 1:7*

Debilitating fear is not from the Lord. We can call upon God's Spirit to give us the power to face our foes, the love to overcome evil with good, and the discipline to persevere through our trials. We have been given the power to turn from fear to faith.

How can I confront fear?

What can we say about such wonderful things as these? If God is for us, who can ever be against us? Since God did not spare even his own Son but gave him up for us all, won't God, who gave us Christ, also give us everything else? *ROMANS 8:31-32*

Don't be afraid, for I am with you. Do not be dismayed, for I am your God. I will strengthen you. I will help you. I will uphold you with my victorious right hand. *ISAIAH 41:10*

God's presence calms our panic. God's care is the antidote to our despair. God's power resolves our problems.

FELLOWSHIP

How does the Lord change the quality of our fellowship?

Where two or three gather together because they are mine, I am there among them. *MATTHEW 18:20*

The promise of the Lord's presence transforms our fellowship. We draw strength from the testimony of God's faithfulness in others' lives. We learn to comfort one another with the comfort we receive from the Lord. And we experience love and forgiveness in practical ways.

What does God promise when we make healthy fellowship a priority?

All of you should be of one mind, full of sympathy toward each other, loving one another with tender hearts and humble minds. Don't repay evil for evil. Don't retaliate when people say unkind things about you. Instead, pay them back with a blessing. That is what God wants you to do, and he will bless you for it. *1 PETER 3:8-9*

Do any of you want to live a life that is long and good? Then watch your tongue! Keep your lips from telling lies! Turn away from evil and do good. Work hard at living in peace with others. The eyes of the LORD watch over those who do right; his ears are open to their cries for help. *PSALM 34:12-15*

FORGIVENESS

What happens when I confess my sin?

He forgives all my sins and heals all my diseases … He has not punished us for all our sins, nor does he deal with us as we deserve. For his unfailing love toward those who fear him is as great as the height of the heavens above the earth. He has removed our rebellious acts as far away from us as the east is from the west. PSALM 103:3, 10-12

This is my blood, which seals the covenant between God and his people. It is poured out to forgive the sins of many. MATTHEW 26:28

Jesus gave his life so that we could be forgiven and reconciled to God. When we put our trust in him, he pays our debt in full.

Do I have to forgive others who hurt me?

If you forgive those who sin against you, your heavenly Father will forgive you. But if you refuse to forgive others, your Father will not forgive your sins. MATTHEW 6:14-15

Peter came to him and asked, "Lord, how often should I forgive someone who sins against me? Seven times?" "No!" Jesus replied, "seventy times seven!" MATTHEW 18:21-22

Just as God forgives us without limit, we should forgive others without keeping score.

FUTURE

How can hope for the future help me live today?

What we suffer now is nothing compared to the glory he will give us later. For all creation is waiting eagerly for that future day when God will reveal who his children really are. Against its will, everything on earth was subjected to God's curse. All creation anticipates the day when it will join God's children in glorious freedom from death and decay. For we know that all creation has been groaning as in the pains of childbirth right up to the present time. And even we Christians, although we have the Holy Spirit within us as a foretaste of future glory, also groan to be released from pain and suffering. We, too, wait anxiously for that day when God will give us our full rights as his children, including the new bodies he has promised us. Now that we are saved, we eagerly look forward to this freedom. For if you already have something, you don't need to hope for it. But if we look forward to something we don't have yet, we must wait patiently and confidently. ROMANS 8:18-25

We have strength and courage to face the trials and suffering of this life because we can look beyond them to the glory that God has in store for us.

The LORD says, "I will guide you along the best pathway for your life. I will advise you and watch over you." PSALM 32:8

GIVING

How does giving to others affect my own life?

I have been a constant example of how you can help the poor by working hard. You should remember the words of the Lord Jesus: "It is more blessed to give than to receive." *ACTS 20:35*

If you give, you will receive. Your gift will return to you in full measure, pressed down, shaken together to make room for more, and running over. Whatever measure you use in giving—large or small—it will be used to measure what is given back to you. *LUKE 6:38*

All goes well for those who are generous, who lend freely and conduct their business fairly. Such people will not be overcome by evil circumstances. Those who are righteous will be long remembered. *PSALM 112:5-6*

If you give even a cup of cold water to one of the least of my followers, you will surely be rewarded. *MATTHEW 10:42*

What if I don't seem to have enough to give?

God will generously provide all you need. Then you will always have everything you need and plenty left over to share with others. *2 CORINTHIANS 9:8*

Give generously, for your gifts will return to you later. *ECCLESIASTES 11:1*

GRACE

What is grace?

God saved you by his special favor when you believed. And you can't take credit for this; it is a gift from God. Salvation is not a reward for the good things we have done, so none of us can boast about it. *EPHESIANS 2:8-9*

Grace is God's special favor.

The wages of sin is death, but the free gift of God is eternal life through Christ Jesus our Lord. *ROMANS 6:23*

When the Bible says we are saved by grace, it means that God has freely chosen to pardon our sin through Jesus Christ. We do not have to earn God's love or work our way to heaven. By grace, we are forgiven for our sin and restored to full fellowship with God.

How does grace affect my daily life?

Sin is no longer your master, for you are no longer subject to the law, which enslaves you to sin. Instead, you are free by God's grace. *ROMANS 6:14*

The LORD is merciful and gracious; he is slow to get angry and full of unfailing love. *PSALM 103:8*

What we believe about God is the most important thing about us. When we believe the depth of his love and grace toward us, we enter into joy and freedom.

The wages of sin is death, but the free *gift* of God is eternal *life* through Christ Jesus our Lord.

Romans 6:23

GUIDANCE

How can I be sure God will guide me?

The LORD says, "I will guide you along the best pathway for your life. I will advise you and watch over you." PSALM 32:8

The steps of the godly are directed by the LORD. He delights in every detail of their lives. Though they stumble, they will not fall, for the LORD holds them by the hand. PSALM 37:23-24

"I know the plans I have for you," says the LORD. "They are plans for good and not for disaster, to give you a future and a hope." JEREMIAH 29:11

How can I experience God's guidance?

Keep on asking, and you will be given what you ask for. Keep on looking, and you will find. Keep on knocking, and the door will be opened. For everyone who asks, receives. Everyone who seeks, finds. And the door is opened to everyone who knocks. You parents—if your children ask for a loaf of bread, do you give them a stone instead? Or if they ask for a fish, do you give them a snake? Of course not! If you sinful people know how to give good gifts to your children, how much more will your heavenly Father give good gifts to those who ask him. MATTHEW 7:7-11

HABITS

How can God help me deal with bad habits?

Those who are dominated by the sinful nature think about sinful things, but those who are controlled by the Holy Spirit think about things that please the Spirit. If your sinful nature controls your mind, there is death. But if the Holy Spirit controls your mind, there is life and peace. *ROMANS 8:5-6*

Do not let sin control the way you live; do not give in to its lustful desires. Do not let any part of your body become a tool of wickedness, to be used for sinning. Instead, give yourselves completely to God since you have been given new life. And use your whole body as a tool to do what is right for the glory of God. Sin is no longer your master, for you are no longer subject to the law, which enslaves you to sin. Instead, you are free by God's grace. *ROMANS 6:12-14*

How can God help me cultivate good habits?

Do not waste time arguing over godless ideas and old wives' tales. Spend your time and energy in training yourself for spiritual fitness. Physical exercise has some value, but spiritual exercise is much more important, for it promises a reward in both this life and the next. *1 TIMOTHY 4:7-8*

HEALING

Does God heal us?

If you will listen carefully to the voice of the LORD your God and do what is right in his sight, obeying his commands and laws, then I will not make you suffer the diseases I sent on the Egyptians; for I am the LORD who heals you. *EXODUS 15:26*

God can overcome any threat in our lives—physical, mental, spiritual, or emotional.

For you who fear my name, the Sun of Righteousness will rise with healing in his wings. And you will go free, leaping with joy like calves let out to pasture. *MALACHI 4:2*

God's healing can reach every level of our lives. His healing brings a joy and freedom that cannot be contained.

How can I seek God's healing?

He forgives all my sins and heals all my diseases. *PSALM 103:3*

Sin can make us sick, literally. Healing can come if we repent of our sin and receive God's forgiveness.

I will never forget your commandments, for you have used them to restore my joy and health. *PSALM 119:93*

Following God's direction can bring healing in our lives. God's word shows us how to break free from the stress, the pressure, and the unhealthy practices that undermine our health.

God so *loved* the world that he *gave* his only Son, so that everyone who believes in him will not perish but have ETERNAL LIFE.

John 3:16

HEAVEN

Is there really a heaven?

For we know that when this earthly tent we live in is taken down—when we die and leave these bodies—we will have a home in heaven, an eternal body made for us by God himself and not by human hands. *2 CORINTHIANS 5:1*

Heaven is described most often in terms of being our home. It is not a paradise we will simply visit on vacation, but an eternal dwelling place where we will live in joyful fellowship with our heavenly Father and his family.

How can I be certain I will go to heaven?

Because God's children are human beings—made of flesh and blood—Jesus also became flesh and blood by being born in human form. For only as a human being could he die, and only by dying could he break the power of the Devil, who had the power of death. Only in this way could he deliver those who have lived all their lives as slaves to the fear of dying *HEBREWS 2:14-15*

God so loved the world that he gave his only Son, so that everyone who believes in him will not perish but have eternal life. *JOHN 3:16*

HOLY

How is it possible for me to be holy?

Long ago, even before he made the world, God loved us and chose us in Christ to be holy and without fault in his eyes.

EPHESIANS 1:4

God alone made it possible for you to be in Christ Jesus. For our benefit God made Christ to be wisdom itself. He is the one who made us acceptable to God. He made us pure and holy, and he gave himself to purchase our freedom.

1 CORINTHIANS 1:30

We are brought into a state of holiness not by what we do, but by what Jesus did for us, cleansing and forgiving us from sin.

How can my life become more holy?

Now I entrust you to God and the word of his grace— his message that is able to build you up and give you an inheritance with all those he has set apart for himself.

ACTS 20:32

Make them pure and holy by teaching them your words of truth. *JOHN 17:17*

Jesus' prayer for us assures us that God will do everything possible to bring us to holiness. God's word both instructs and inspires us to become holy and mature in our faith.

HOLY SPIRIT

When do I receive the Holy Spirit?

Now you also have heard the truth, the Good News that God saves you. And when you believed in Christ, he identified you as his own by giving you the Holy Spirit, whom he promised long ago. The Spirit is God's guarantee that he will give us everything he promised and that he has purchased us to be his own people. This is just one more reason for us to praise our glorious God. EPHESIANS 1:13-14

God gives us the Holy Spirit when we believe in Jesus Christ. Some would even say that God gives us the Holy Spirit to enable us to believe in Christ.

How does the Holy Spirit help me?

The Holy Spirit helps us in our distress. For we don't even know what we should pray for, nor how we should pray. But the Holy Spirit prays for us with groanings that cannot be expressed in words. And the Father who knows all hearts knows what the Spirit is saying, for the Spirit pleads for us believers in harmony with God's own will. ROMANS 8:26-27

Don't you know that your body is the temple of the Holy Spirit, who lives in you and was given to you by God? You do not belong to yourself. 1 CORINTHIANS 6:19

I pray that God,
who gives you *hope*,
will keep you happy
and full of *peace*
as you believe
in him.

Romans 15:13

HOPE

What is my hope?

Through Christ you have come to trust in God. And because God raised Christ from the dead and gave him great glory, your faith and hope can be placed confidently in God.
1 PETER 1:21

The resurrection, the greatest event in history, is the foundation of our hope.

How can I have hope when times are tough?

Without wavering, let us hold tightly to the hope we say we have, for God can be trusted to keep his promise.
HEBREWS 10:23

Don't be troubled. You trust God, now trust in me. *JOHN 14:1*

I have told you all this so that you may have peace in me. Here on earth you will have many trials and sorrows. But take heart, because I have overcome the world. *JOHN 16:33*

Our troubles do not surprise the Lord and should not surprise us. Trouble is rampant in this fallen world. Our focus should be on Jesus who has overcome this world and all its troubles.

I pray that God, who gives you hope, will keep you happy and full of peace as you believe in him. May you overflow with hope through the power of the Holy Spirit. *ROMANS 15:13*

HUMILITY

How does God respond to the humble?

He leads the humble in what is right, teaching them his way.
PSALM 25:9

Humility means acknowledging our proper place before the Lord. When we humbly worship him, he will lead us and teach us the right way to live.

The LORD delights in his people; he crowns the humble with salvation. PSALM 149:4

Those who exalt themselves will be humbled, and those who humble themselves will be exalted. MATTHEW 23:12

Though the LORD is great, he cares for the humble, but he keeps his distance from the proud. PSALM 138:6

Anyone who becomes as humble as this little child is the greatest in the Kingdom of Heaven. MATTHEW 18:4

Humble yourselves under the mighty power of God, and in his good time he will honor you. Give all your worries and cares to God, for he cares about what happens to you.
1 PETER 5:6-7

The less we try to honor ourselves, the more God honors and blesses us. Pride builds barriers that keep God out of our lives. Humility opens the way for God to work because we are more willing to seek God's help and honor him for helping.

HUNGER FOR GOD

How does God respond to my hunger and longing?

He satisfies the thirsty and fills the hungry with good things.
PSALM 107:9

Jesus replied, "I am the bread of life. No one who comes to me will ever be hungry again. Those who believe in me will never thirst." JOHN 6:35

How can I satisfy the deep longings of my life?

Don't worry about having enough food or drink or clothing. Why be like the pagans who are so deeply concerned about these things? Your heavenly Father already knows all your needs, and he will give you all you need from day to day if you live for him and make the Kingdom of God your primary concern. MATTHEW 6:31-33

When we seek the Lord and order our lives according to his priorities, everything else falls into proper perspective.

Take delight in the LORD, and he will give you your heart's desires. Commit everything you do to the LORD. Trust him, and he will help you. PSALM 37:4-5

Faith does not mean inaction. The Lord invites us to earnestly pursue our godly desires. As we do, he promises to lead us into joy and satisfaction.

INSECURITY

How can I find security in who I am?

The LORD your God has arrived to live among you. He is a mighty savior. He will rejoice over you with great gladness. With his love, he will calm all your fears. He will exult over you by singing a happy song. *ZEPHANIAH 3:17*

You are the salt of the earth. But what good is salt if it has lost its flavor? Can you make it useful again? It will be thrown out and trampled underfoot as worthless. You are the light of the world—like a city on a mountain, glowing in the night for all to see. Don't hide your light under a basket! Instead, put it on a stand and let it shine for all. In the same way, let your good deeds shine out for all to see, so that everyone will praise your heavenly Father. *MATTHEW 5:13-16*

How does God protect me?

My sheep recognize my voice; I know them, and they follow me. I give them eternal life, and they will never perish. No one will snatch them away from me, for my Father has given them to me, and he is more powerful than anyone else. So no one can take them from me. The Father and I are one.

JOHN 10:27-30

INTEGRITY

What are the benefits of integrity?

Good people are guided by their honesty; treacherous people are destroyed by their dishonesty ... The godly are directed by their honesty; the wicked fall beneath their load of sin. *PROVERBS 11:3, 5*

Integrity keeps us from the trap of dishonesty and the destruction that can result.

Be careful how you live among your unbelieving neighbors. Even if they accuse you of doing wrong, they will see your honorable behavior, and they will believe and give honor to God when he comes to judge the world. *1 PETER 2:12*

Our integrity may not bring immediate rewards, but we are certain that it will one day be recognized.

How does the Lord enable us to seek integrity?

My child, listen to me and treasure my instructions. Tune your ears to wisdom, and concentrate on understanding ... Then you will understand what it means to fear the LORD, and you will gain knowledge of God ... Then you will understand what is right, just, and fair, and you will know how to find the right course of action every time. *PROVERBS 2:1-2, 5, 9*

God has given us the wisdom we need to lead lives that honor him. His word gives us the understanding, discernment, and motivation to choose the way of integrity.

JESUS CHRIST

Who is Jesus Christ?

Jesus Christ, the Son of God, never wavers between yes and no. He is the one whom Timothy, Silas, and I preached to you, and he is the divine Yes—God's affirmation. For all of God's promises have been fulfilled in him. That is why we say "Amen" when we give glory to God through Christ. *2 CORINTHIANS 1:19-20*

What has Jesus promised to those who believe in him?

To all who believed him and accepted him, he gave the right to become children of God. *JOHN 1:12*

The thief's purpose is to steal and kill and destroy. My purpose is to give life in all its fullness. *JOHN 10:10*

We also pray that you will be strengthened with his glorious power so that you will have all the patience and endurance you need. May you be filled with joy, always thanking the Father, who has enabled you to share the inheritance that belongs to God's holy people, who live in the light. For he has rescued us from the one who rules in the kingdom of darkness, and he has brought us into the Kingdom of his dear Son. God has purchased our freedom with his blood and has forgiven all our sins. *COLOSSIANS 1:11-14*

JOY

Where does joy come from?

Nehemiah continued, "Go and celebrate with a feast of choice foods and sweet drinks, and share gifts of food with people who have nothing prepared. This is a sacred day before our Lord. Don't be dejected and sad, for the joy of the LORD is your strength!" *NEHEMIAH 8:10*

Our joy springs from God's love, which is not dependent on circumstances nor on our performance. When we trust in his love for us, we are far less vulnerable to the depression and despair that could come from our problems and disappointments.

How can I be joyful in hard times?

Even though the fig trees have no blossoms, and there are no grapes on the vine; even though the olive crop fails, and the fields lie empty and barren; even though the flocks die in the fields, and the cattle barns are empty, yet I will rejoice in the LORD! I will be joyful in the God of my salvation.
HABAKKUK 3:17-18

Joy is a choice. We may not realize it, but we choose our moods and our attitudes. God's promises in Christ are the basis for choosing joy no matter what we face.

The *joy* of
the LORD is your
STRENGTH!

Nehemiah 8:10

JUDGMENT

How will I be able to face the judgment of God?

Since we have been made right in God's sight by the blood of Christ, he will certainly save us from God's judgment. For since we were restored to friendship with God by the death of his Son while we were still his enemies, we will certainly be delivered from eternal punishment by his life. ROMANS 5:9-10

Jesus has relieved us from the threat of condemnation and death.

How does the future judgment affect my life now?

No one can lay any other foundation than the one we already have—Jesus Christ. Now anyone who builds on that foundation may use gold, silver, jewels, wood, hay, or straw. But there is going to come a time of testing at the judgment day to see what kind of work each builder has done. Everyone's work will be put through the fire to see whether or not it keeps its value. If the work survives the fire, that builder will receive a reward. But if the work is burned up, the builder will suffer great loss. The builders themselves will be saved, but like someone escaping through a wall of flames. 1 CORINTHIANS 3:11-15

The promise of salvation does not eliminate our responsibility. God has given us all that is necessary to lead meaningful, spiritually productive lives. We ignore his promises and provisions at great risk.

JUSTICE

What can I do when I suffer injustice?

Never pay back evil for evil to anyone. Do things in such a way that everyone can see you are honorable. Do your part to live in peace with everyone, as much as possible. Dear friends, never avenge yourselves. Leave that to God. For it is written, "I will take vengeance; I will repay those who deserve it," says the Lord. *ROMANS 12:17-19*

Don't say, "I will get even for this wrong." Wait for the LORD to handle the matter. *PROVERBS 20:22*

God teaches us to respond differently to injustice than the world does. Vengeance and retribution are the way of the world. God teaches us to trust in him and allow him to settle the score.

How can I respond to persecution?

God blesses you when you are mocked and persecuted and lied about because you are my followers. Be happy about it! Be very glad! For a great reward awaits you in heaven. And remember, the ancient prophets were persecuted, too. *MATTHEW 5:11-12*

God will use this persecution to show his justice. For he will make you worthy of his Kingdom, for which you are suffering, and in his justice he will punish those who persecute you. *2 THESSALONIANS 1:5-6*

LOVE

What are the benefits of loving God?

Understand, therefore, that the LORD your God is indeed God. He is the faithful God who keeps his covenant for a thousand generations and constantly loves those who love him and obey his commands. *DEUTERONOMY 7:9*

This promise comforts us and inspires increasing gratitude and commitment to our gracious Lord. God's love and devotion literally reach across time to multiple generations.

What are the benefits of loving others?

God is not unfair. He will not forget how hard you have worked for him and how you have shown your love to him by caring for other Christians, as you still do. *HEBREWS 6:10*

Those who live only to satisfy their own sinful desires will harvest the consequences of decay and death. But those who live to please the Spirit will harvest everlasting life from the Spirit. So don't get tired of doing what is good. Don't get discouraged and give up, for we will reap a harvest of blessing at the appropriate time. Whenever we have the opportunity, we should do good to everyone, especially to our Christian brothers and sisters. *GALATIANS 6:8-10*

The Holy Spirit awakens our love for others. We can ask God to make us willing to love others—even those who are difficult—and God will hear our prayer.

LOVE OF GOD

How can I know God really loves me?

See how very much our heavenly Father loves us, for he allows us to be called his children, and we really are! But the people who belong to this world don't know God, so they don't understand that we are his children. *1 JOHN 3:1*

We know how dearly God loves us, because he has given us the Holy Spirit to fill our hearts with his love. *ROMANS 5:5*

What are the benefits of God's love for me?

Surely your goodness and unfailing love will pursue me all the days of my life, and I will live in the house of the LORD forever. *PSALM 23:6*

We can be certain that God will continually shower us with his mercy and guard us in his love.

I am overcome with joy because of your unfailing love, for you have seen my troubles, and you care about the anguish of my soul. *PSALM 31:7*

God understands our weaknesses and struggles without condemning us.

The LORD is merciful and gracious; he is slow to get angry and full of unfailing love. *PSALM 103:8*

Honor the LORD with your *wealth* and with the best part of everything your land produces. Then he will *fill* your barns with grain, and your vats will *overflow* with the finest wine.

Proverbs 3:9-10

MINISTRY

What is God calling me to do?

He said to his disciples, "The harvest is so great, but the workers are so few." *MATTHEW 9:37*

People are ready to hear and receive the Good News of God's love. But with this promise comes the responsibility to work and to pray.

How do I know God will help me minister for him?

When the Holy Spirit has come upon you, you will receive power and will tell people about me everywhere—in Jerusalem, throughout Judea, in Samaria, and to the ends of the earth. *ACTS 1:8*

There are different kinds of spiritual gifts, but it is the same Holy Spirit who is the source of them all. There are different kinds of service in the church, but it is the same Lord we are serving. There are different ways God works in our lives, but it is the same God who does the work through all of us. A spiritual gift is given to each of us as a means of helping the entire church. *1 CORINTHIANS 12:4-7*

God has given every believer the gift of the Holy Spirit, and the Holy Spirit gives us his gifts as well. Great joy is ours as we share God's gifts with others.

MONEY

Will God provide for my financial needs?

Don't worry about having enough food or drink or clothing. Why be like the pagans who are so deeply concerned about these things? Your heavenly Father already knows all your needs, and he will give you all you need from day to day if you live for him and make the Kingdom of God your primary concern. *MATTHEW 6:31-33*

God knows our needs and promises to supply them fully.

What are the benefits of using my money as God directs?

Honor the LORD with your wealth and with the best part of everything your land produces. Then he will fill your barns with grain, and your vats will overflow with the finest wine. *PROVERBS 3:9-10*

We do not give in order to get, but we will often get when we give. When we are generous toward others, God is generous toward us.

Stay away from the love of money; be satisfied with what you have. For God has said, "I will never fail you. I will never forsake you." *HEBREWS 13:5*

It is possible to give freely and become more wealthy, but those who are stingy will lose everything. *PROVERBS 11:24*

NEEDS

How can I be sure my needs will be met?

The Lord is my shepherd; I have everything I need. *PSALM 23:1*

What can we say about such wonderful things as these? If God is for us, who can ever be against us? Since God did not spare even his own Son but gave him up for us all, won't God, who gave us Christ, also give us everything else? *ROMANS 8:31-32*

God has met our greatest need by giving us his own Son to redeem us.

This same God who takes care of me will supply all your needs from his glorious riches, which have been given to us in Christ Jesus. *PHILIPPIANS 4:19*

God's resources far exceed my greatest needs.

Let us come boldly to the throne of our gracious God. There we will receive his mercy, and we will find grace to help us when we need it. *HEBREWS 4:16*

Why does God promise to meet my needs?

He will give you all you need from day to day if you live for him and make the Kingdom of God your primary concern. *MATTHEW 6:33*

God will generously provide all you need. Then you will always have everything you need and plenty left over to share with others. *2 CORINTHIANS 9:8*

OBEDIENCE

Why is obedience important to my spiritual life?

If you will obey me and keep my covenant, you will be my own special treasure from among all the nations of the earth; for all the earth belongs to me. *EXODUS 19:5*

This is what I told them: "Obey me, and I will be your God, and you will be my people. Only do as I say, and all will be well!" *JEREMIAH 7:23*

What does God promise to those who obey?

The LORD God is our light and protector. He gives us grace and glory. No good thing will the LORD withhold from those who do what is right. *PSALM 84:11*

If you love me, obey my commandments. And I will ask the Father, and he will give you another Counselor, who will never leave you. He is the Holy Spirit, who leads into all truth. The world at large cannot receive him, because it isn't looking for him and doesn't recognize him. But you do, because he lives with you now and later will be in you. *JOHN 14:15-17*

The power God gives us is his own Holy Spirit, our Counselor. He comes alongside us to advise us, inspire us, and actually live and work through us.

OPPORTUNITIES

How can I face challenging, sometimes intimidating, opportunities?

I can do everything with the help of Christ who gives me the strength I need. *PHILIPPIANS 4:13*

Our ability to face challenges is rooted in Christ, not in ourselves. With Christ's help, we can make the most of every opportunity.

I know all the things you do, and I have opened a door for you that no one can shut. You have little strength, yet you obeyed my word and did not deny me. *REVELATION 3:8*

We can trust that nothing will prevent us from fulfilling the opportunity God has for us.

How do I know if an opportunity is from the Lord?

Be strong and very courageous. Obey all the laws Moses gave you. Do not turn away from them, and you will be successful in everything you do. Study this Book of the Law continually. Meditate on it day and night so you may be sure to obey all that is written in it. Only then will you succeed. I command you—be strong and courageous! Do not be afraid or discouraged. For the LORD your God is with you wherever you go. *JOSHUA 1:7-9*

PATIENCE

Where do I find the resources to be patient?

When the Holy Spirit controls our lives, he will produce this kind of fruit in us: love, joy, peace, patience, kindness, goodness, faithfulness. *GALATIANS 5:22*

We also pray that you will be strengthened with his glorious power so that you will have all the patience and endurance you need. May you be filled with joy. *COLOSSIANS 1:11*

We can rejoice, too, when we run into problems and trials, for we know that they are good for us—they help us learn to endure. And endurance develops strength of character in us, and character strengthens our confident expectation of salvation. And this expectation will not disappoint us. For we know how dearly God loves us, because he has given us the Holy Spirit to fill our hearts with his love. *ROMANS 5:3-5*

What happens when I am patient?

Those who wait on the LORD will find new strength. They will fly high on wings like eagles. They will run and not grow weary. They will walk and not faint. *ISAIAH 40:31*

Patient endurance is what you need now, so you will continue to do God's will. Then you will receive all that he has promised. *HEBREWS 10:36*

Those who give up, lose out. They are not being punished for giving up; they simply are absent when God works.

PEACE

How can I find peace within?

I am leaving you with a gift—peace of mind and heart. And the peace I give isn't like the peace the world gives. So don't be troubled or afraid. *JOHN 14:27*

The LORD gives his people strength. The LORD blesses them with peace. *PSALM 29:11*

I will lie down in peace and sleep, for you alone, O LORD, will keep me safe. *PSALM 4:8*

Don't worry about anything; instead, pray about everything. Tell God what you need, and thank him for all he has done. If you do this, you will experience God's peace, which is far more wonderful than the human mind can understand. His peace will guard your hearts and minds as you live in Christ Jesus. *PHILIPPIANS 4:6-7*

You will keep in perfect peace all who trust in you, whose thoughts are fixed on you! *ISAIAH 26:3*

I am leaving you with a gift—peace of mind and heart. And the peace I give isn't like the peace the world gives. So don't be troubled or afraid. *JOHN 14:27*

I will lie down
in *peace* and sleep,
for you alone,
O LORD,
will keep me *safe*.

Psalm 4:8

PLANNING

How am I supposed to plan my life?

Trust in the LORD with all your heart; do not depend on your own understanding. Seek his will in all you do, and he will direct your paths. *PROVERBS 3:5-6*

As we seek God, he will guide us in making our plans.

You can make many plans, but the Lord's purpose will prevail. *PROVERBS 19:21*

Our plans cannot mess up God's plans!

What gives me confidence in any plans?

God's secret plan has now been revealed to us; it is a plan centered on Christ, designed long ago according to his good pleasure. And this is his plan: At the right time he will bring everything together under the authority of Christ— everything in heaven and on earth. *EPHESIANS 1:9-10*

God is in control of all things and always has been. Jesus Christ, who is now resurrected and ruling, will govern and guide us in the best possible ways.

"I know the plans I have for you," says the LORD. "They are plans for good and not for disaster, to give you a future and a hope." *JEREMIAH 29:11*

Do not doubt God's good intentions for us.

POWER OF GOD

What is God's power like?

You are my King and my God. You command victories for your people. Only by your power can we push back our enemies; only in your name can we trample our foes. I do not trust my bow; I do not count on my sword to save me. It is you who gives us victory over our enemies; it is you who humbles those who hate us. *PSALM 44:4-7*

God's power is greater than any of the skills or resources we have at our disposal. While we may use the means that God has provided to us, we know that victory comes from God alone.

How can God's power help me?

With God's help we will do mighty things, for he will trample down our foes. *PSALM 60:12*

He gives power to those who are tired and worn out; he offers strength to the weak. *ISAIAH 40:29*

God, in his mighty power, will protect you until you receive this salvation, because you are trusting him. It will be revealed on the last day for all to see. *1 PETER 1:5*

God is working in you, giving you the desire to obey him and the power to do what pleases him. *PHILIPPIANS 2:13*

PRAYER

How can I know God hears my prayers?

The LORD is close to all who call on him, yes, to all who call on him sincerely. *PSALM 145:18*

The eyes of the Lord watch over those who do right, and his ears are open to their prayers. But the Lord turns his face against those who do evil. *1 PETER 3:12*

Since prayer is a conversation with God, we must approach God with the same love and courtesy we bring to any relationship we value. We must be humble, not arrogant. We must admit our sin and seek God's forgiveness.

How will God respond to my prayers?

Give all your worries and cares to God, for he cares about what happens to you. *1 PETER 5:7*

We experience freedom when we give a burden over to the Lord in prayer—even before the prayer is answered. The assurance of God's love and concern refreshes us and renews our hope.

Don't worry about anything; instead, pray about everything. Tell God what you need, and thank him for all he has done. If you do this, you will experience God's peace, which is far more wonderful than the human mind can understand. His peace will guard your hearts and minds as you live in Christ Jesus. *PHILIPPIANS 4:6-7*

PRESENCE OF GOD

Are there times or places when God leaves me?

I command you—be strong and courageous! Do not be afraid or discouraged. For the LORD your God is with you wherever you go. *JOSHUA 1:9*

Teach these new disciples to obey all the commands I have given you. And be sure of this: I am with you always, even to the end of the age. *MATTHEW 28:20*

I know the LORD is always with me. I will not be shaken, for he is right beside me … You will show me the way of life, granting me the joy of your presence and the pleasures of living with you forever. *PSALM 16:8, 11*

When you go through deep waters and great trouble, I will be with you. When you go through rivers of difficulty, you will not drown! When you walk through the fire of oppression, you will not be burned up; the flames will not consume you. *ISAIAH 43:2*

How can we experience God's presence?

The LORD is close to all who call on him, yes, to all who call on him sincerely. *PSALM 145:18*

Draw close to God, and God will draw close to you. Wash your hands, you sinners; purify your hearts, you hypocrites. *JAMES 4:8*

PROBLEMS

What do I do when problems overwhelm me?

We are pressed on every side by troubles, but we are not crushed and broken. We are perplexed, but we don't give up and quit. We are hunted down, but God never abandons us. We get knocked down, but we get up again and keep going. Through suffering, these bodies of ours constantly share in the death of Jesus so that the life of Jesus may also be seen in our bodies. *2 CORINTHIANS 4:8-10*

He orders his angels to protect you wherever you go. *PSALM 91:11*

Angels are only servants. They are spirits sent from God to care for those who will receive salvation. *HEBREWS 1:14*

In addition to all the other sources of help, God sends his mighty angels to watch over us. Though we rarely see them, we can trust God's word that they will care for us.

How can we help each other with our problems?

Share each other's troubles and problems, and in this way obey the law of Christ. *GALATIANS 6:2*

While we each have burdens to bear, one of the great advantages of being a part of God's family is that we do not have to bear our burdens alone.

He orders

his *angels* to

PROTECT

you wherever you go.

Psalm 91:11

PROPHECY

What promises does God have for our future?

Then at last, the sign of the coming of the Son of Man will appear in the heavens, and there will be deep mourning among all the nations of the earth. And they will see the Son of Man arrive on the clouds of heaven with power and great glory. And he will send forth his angels with the sound of a mighty trumpet blast, and they will gather together his chosen ones from the farthest ends of the earth and heaven.

MATTHEW 24:30-31

I can tell you this directly from the Lord: We who are still living when the Lord returns will not rise to meet him ahead of those who are in their graves. For the Lord himself will come down from heaven with a commanding shout, with the call of the archangel, and with the trumpet call of God. First, all the Christians who have died will rise from their graves. Then, together with them, we who are still alive and remain on the earth will be caught up in the clouds to meet the Lord in the air and remain with him forever. So comfort and encourage each other with these words.

1 THESSALONIANS 4:15-18

One of the greatest promises in the Bible is that Jesus will come again.

PROTECTION

Where can I find protection and safety?

My help comes from the LORD, who made the heavens and the earth! He will not let you stumble and fall; the one who watches over you will not sleep. Indeed, he who watches over Israel never tires and never sleeps. The LORD himself watches over you! The LORD stands beside you as your protective shade. The sun will not hurt you by day, nor the moon at night. The LORD keeps you from all evil and preserves your life. The LORD keeps watch over you as you come and go, both now and forever. *PSALM 121:2-8*

The LORD is a shelter for the oppressed, a refuge in times of trouble. *PSALM 9:9*

How does the Lord protect me?

Be strong with the Lord's mighty power. Put on all of God's armor so that you will be able to stand firm against all strategies and tricks of the Devil. For we are not fighting against people made of flesh and blood, but against the evil rulers and authorities of the unseen world, against those mighty powers of darkness who rule this world, and against wicked spirits in the heavenly realms. *EPHESIANS 6:10-12*

PROVISION

Can I expect God to supply my needs?

Trust me in your times of trouble, and I will rescue you, and you will give me glory. *PSALM 50:15*

This same God who takes care of me will supply all your needs from his glorious riches, which have been given to us in Christ Jesus. *PHILIPPIANS 4:19*

How is Jesus Christ God's provision for me?

I am the good shepherd; I know my own sheep, and they know me, just as my Father knows me and I know the Father. And I lay down my life for the sheep. *JOHN 10:14-15*

I am the true vine, and my Father is the gardener ... Yes, I am the vine; you are the branches. Those who remain in me, and I in them, will produce much fruit. For apart from me you can do nothing ... If you stay joined to me and my words remain in you, you may ask any request you like, and it will be granted! My true disciples produce much fruit. This brings great glory to my Father. *JOHN 15:1, 5, 7-8*

Jesus is God's greatest provision for our greatest needs.

PURPOSE

Does God have a purpose for my life?

It is God who saved us and chose us to live a holy life. He did this not because we deserved it, but because that was his plan long before the world began—to show his love and kindness to us through Christ Jesus. *2 TIMOTHY 1:9*

You didn't choose me. I chose you. I appointed you to go and produce fruit that will last, so that the Father will give you whatever you ask for, using my name. *JOHN 15:16*

How can I discover my purpose and fulfill it?

I live in eager expectation and hope that I will never do anything that causes me shame, but that I will always be bold for Christ, as I have been in the past, and that my life will always honor Christ, whether I live or I die. For to me, living is for Christ, and dying is even better. Yet if I live, that means fruitful service for Christ. I really don't know which is better. *PHILIPPIANS 1:20-22*

When we commit ourselves to fulfilling God's purpose for our lives, the Lord promises that our lives will be fruitful. We will find meaning for ourselves and lead others to know the truth of Jesus Christ.

RENEWAL

How can I find spiritual renewal

Create in me a clean heart, O God. Renew a right spirit within me ... Restore to me again the joy of your salvation, and make me willing to obey you. *PSALM 51:10, 12*

Sometimes we are weary because we cling to sin and disobedience. Renewal comes through confession, repentance, and God's forgiving grace.

I will give you a new heart with new and right desires, and I will put a new spirit in you. I will take out your stony heart of sin and give you a new, obedient heart. And I will put my Spirit in you so you will obey my laws and do whatever I command. *EZEKIEL 36:26-27*

Renewal comes from a new heart and from the Holy Spirit. What was promised to Ezekiel was fulfilled in Christ.

How can I experience spiritual renewal on a more frequent, even continual, basis?

He renews my strength. He guides me along right paths, bringing honor to his name. *PSALM 23:3*

God promises us spiritual refreshment if we dwell in his presence daily. Peace, confidence, and energy flow naturally from fellowship with the Lord.

He *renews* my
STRENGTH.
He *guides* me
along right paths,
bringing honor
to his name.

Psalm 23:3

REPUTATION

Does God care about my reputation?

Work hard and cheerfully at whatever you do, as though you were working for the Lord rather than for people. Remember that the Lord will give you an inheritance as your reward, and the Master you are serving is Christ. COLOSSIANS 3:23-24

What matters most is not what others think of us, but what God thinks of us (see Galatians 1:10). When we seek to please the Lord, he will give us favor with others.

How can I maintain a godly reputation?

Never let loyalty and kindness get away from you! Wear them like a necklace; write them deep within your heart. Then you will find favor with both God and people, and you will gain a good reputation. PROVERBS 3:3-4

Choose a good reputation over great riches, for being held in high esteem is better than having silver or gold. PROVERBS 22:1

God blesses the reputation of those who resist the temptation to trade their name and honor for wealth.

Always be full of joy in the Lord. I say it again—rejoice! Let everyone see that you are considerate in all you do. Remember, the Lord is coming soon. PHILIPPIANS 4:4-5

Joy based on our confidence in Christ makes a powerful—and hopefully eternal—impression on others.

RESCUE

How will God rescue those who depend on him?

Return, O LORD, and rescue me. Save me because of your unfailing love. *PSALM 6:4*

Trust me in your times of trouble, and I will rescue you, and you will give me glory. *PSALM 50:15*

He will rescue the poor when they cry to him; he will help the oppressed, who have no one to defend them. He feels pity for the weak and the needy, and he will rescue them. He will save them from oppression and from violence, for their lives are precious to him. *PSALM 72:12-14*

No situation is too difficult for the Lord. The greater our need, the greater the depth of his love and compassion is for us.

How does God rescue us from the spiritual forces of evil and darkness?

Jesus called his twelve disciples to him and gave them authority to cast out evil spirits and to heal every kind of disease and illness. *MATTHEW 10:1*

Though we are embroiled in a spiritual war with this world, we stand tall because we have full confidence in Christ's authority. We stand strong in the strength and protection of the Lord. This faith overcomes all fear.

REWARDS

Are there rewards in this lifetime for following Jesus?

The LORD God is our light and protector. He gives us grace and glory. No good thing will the LORD withhold from those who do what is right. *PSALM 84:11*

It is impossible to please God without faith. Anyone who wants to come to him must believe that there is a God and that he rewards those who sincerely seek him. *HEBREWS 11:6*

What are the rewards that await us in heaven?

That is what the Scriptures mean when they say, "No eye has seen, no ear has heard, and no mind has imagined what God has prepared for those who love him." *1 CORINTHIANS 2:9*

The best rewards we can imagine pale in comparison with what the Lord has in store for us.

When the head Shepherd comes, your reward will be a never-ending share in his glory and honor. *1 PETER 5:4*

Selfless service brings great rewards.

There is a special rest still waiting for the people of God. *HEBREWS 4:9*

The rest that is promised in heaven is not inactivity. It is the refreshment and satisfaction of savoring a completed, fulfilled work.

SALVATION

What does it mean to be saved?

His unfailing love toward those who fear him is as great as the height of the heavens above the earth. He has removed our rebellious acts as far away from us as the east is from the west. *PSALM 103:11-12*

Being saved means our sins have been completely removed.

Now God in his gracious kindness declares us not guilty. He has done this through Christ Jesus, who has freed us by taking away our sins. *ROMANS 3:24*

God promises to forgive our sins and restore us to full fellowship with him if we put our trust in Jesus Christ. Being saved means no longer having our sins count against us; it means being forgiven by the grace of God and being given eternal life.

How does salvation affect my daily life?

Our old sinful selves were crucified with Christ so that sin might lose its power in our lives. We are no longer slaves to sin. For when we died with Christ we were set free from the power of sin. And since we died with Christ, we know we will also share his new life. *ROMANS 6:6-8*

When the Holy Spirit controls our lives, he will produce this kind of fruit in us: *love*, joy, peace, patience, kindness, *goodness*, faithfulness, gentleness, and self-control. Here there is no conflict with the law.

Galatians 5:22-23

SELF-CONTROL

Is it possible to exercise self-control?

Knowing God leads to self-control. Self-control leads to patient endurance, and patient endurance leads to godliness. *2 PETER 1:6*

Self-control is possible only through God. According to the Bible, sin reigns in our lives, controlling us completely, until Jesus Christ breaks its power.

When the Holy Spirit controls our lives, he will produce this kind of fruit in us: love, joy, peace, patience, kindness, goodness, faithfulness, gentleness, and self-control. Here there is no conflict with the law. *GALATIANS 5:22-23*

What are some steps to exercising self-control?

How can a young person stay pure? By obeying your word and following its rules. *PSALM 119:9*

Do not waste time arguing over godless ideas and old wives' tales. Spend your time and energy in training yourself for spiritual fitness. Physical exercise has some value, but spiritual exercise is much more important, for it promises a reward in both this life and the next. This is true, and everyone should accept it. We work hard and suffer much in order that people will believe the truth, for our hope is in the living God, who is the Savior of all people, and particularly of those who believe. *1 TIMOTHY 4:7-10*

STRENGTH

How can I experience God's strength in my life?

He gives power to those who are tired and worn out; he offers strength to the weak … Those who wait on the LORD will find new strength. They will fly high on wings like eagles. They will run and not grow weary. They will walk and not faint. *ISAIAH 40:29, 31*

Life wears us out, but waiting on the Lord renews our strength. Our limitations remind us to rely more fully on the Lord.

When I pray, you answer me; you encourage me by giving me the strength I need. *PSALM 138:3*

God's strength comes through prayer.

What can I do in God's strength?

I can do everything with the help of Christ who gives me the strength I need. *PHILIPPIANS 4:13*

Now glory be to God! By his mighty power at work within us, he is able to accomplish infinitely more than we would ever dare to ask or hope. *EPHESIANS 3:20*

God is our refuge and strength, always ready to help in times of trouble. So we will not fear, even if earthquakes come and the mountains crumble into the sea. *PSALM 46:1-2*

STRESS

How can I find relief from stress and anxiety?

Jesus said, "Come to me, all of you who are weary and carry heavy burdens, and I will give you rest. Take my yoke upon you. Let me teach you, because I am humble and gentle, and you will find rest for your souls." *MATTHEW 11:28-29*

We can turn from fear and anxiety to faith and peace. God promises to supply the power to get us through the hard times.

What do we learn from stress?

Don't get tired of doing what is good. Don't get discouraged and give up, for we will reap a harvest of blessing at the appropriate time. *GALATIANS 6:9*

We can rejoice, too, when we run into problems and trials, for we know that they are good for us—they help us learn to endure. And endurance develops strength of character in us, and character strengthens our confident expectation of salvation. *ROMANS 5:3-4*

Dear brothers and sisters, whenever trouble comes your way, let it be an opportunity for joy. For when your faith is tested, your endurance has a chance to grow. So let it grow, for when your endurance is fully developed, you will be strong in character and ready for anything. *JAMES 1:2-4*

While stress exposes our true character, it also helps develop our true character.

SUCCESS

Does God promise us success in this life?

The LORD said to Samuel, "Don't judge by his appearance or height, for I have rejected him. The LORD doesn't make decisions the way you do! People judge by outward appearance, but the LORD looks at a person's thoughts and intentions." *1 SAMUEL 16:7*

God's standards differ greatly from our own. Success is measured by faithfulness and fruitfulness not by results and quantities. We measure success in terms of appearances and externals, but the Lord looks on the heart. God measures success by weighing our devotion and commitment to him.

We are confident of all this because of our great trust in God through Christ. It is not that we think we can do anything of lasting value by ourselves. Our only power and success come from God. *2 CORINTHIANS 3:4-5*

Jesus' followers know that real success comes only from the Lord.

How can I pursue success God's way?

Commit your work to the LORD, and then your plans will succeed. *PROVERBS 16:3*

Plans go wrong for lack of advice; many counselors bring success. *PROVERBS 15:22*

SUFFERING

What are God's promises in the midst of suffering?

I am convinced that nothing can ever separate us from his love. Death can't, and life can't. The angels can't, and the demons can't. Our fears for today, our worries about tomorrow, and even the powers of hell can't keep God's love away. Whether we are high above the sky or in the deepest ocean, nothing in all creation will ever be able to separate us from the love of God that is revealed in Christ Jesus our Lord.
ROMANS 8:38-39

The greatest comfort in life is knowing that God will never leave us. Nothing can drive us from his presence. No matter what we are going through, he is there to comfort, sustain, encourage, and direct us.

He heals the brokenhearted, binding up their wounds.
PSALM 147:3

Those who plant in tears will harvest with shouts of joy. They weep as they go to plant their seed, but they sing as they return with the harvest. PSALM 126:5-6

Nothing lasts forever. Sometimes the only thing that keeps us going is the reminder that this time of suffering will also pass. We trust that one day we will look back and it will be a memory. Hopefully, it will also be a testimony to God's faithfulness and a reason for rejoicing.

Humble yourselves before God. Resist the Devil, and he will flee from you.

James 4:7

TEMPTATION

Do I have the power to resist temptation?

Humble yourselves before God. Resist the Devil, and he will flee from you. JAMES 4:7

The devil can tempt us, but we can resist him by responding to the temptation with the truth of God's word.

What steps can I take to resist temptation?

How can a young person stay pure? By obeying your word and following its rules. PSALM 119:9

God's word warns us against evil and shows us the way out of temptation.

Remember that the temptations that come into your life are no different from what others experience. And God is faithful. He will keep the temptation from becoming so strong that you can't stand up against it. When you are tempted, he will show you a way out so that you will not give in to it. 1 CORINTHIANS 10:13

The Lord can lead us away from temptations. He can help us see the deception that blinds us. He can also help us anticipate the terrible consequences that will result from giving in to what we know is wrong. Instead of thinking that we have no chance of resisting, we can call on the Lord to lead us out of temptation.

TIME

How can I best use time?

Teach us to make the most of our time, so that we may grow in wisdom. *PSALM 90:12*

Valuing time begins with seeing it from God's perspective. When we do this, we learn that there is always time for accomplishing God's plans for our lives.

Be careful how you live, not as fools but as those who are wise. Make the most of every opportunity for doing good in these evil days. Don't act thoughtlessly, but try to understand what the Lord wants you to do. Don't be drunk with wine, because that will ruin your life. Instead, let the Holy Spirit fill and control you. Then you will sing psalms and hymns and spiritual songs among yourselves, making music to the Lord in your hearts. And you will always give thanks for everything to God the Father in the name of our Lord Jesus Christ. *EPHESIANS 5:15-20*

Time is a gift. God gives us time so that we have the opportunity to serve him. When we give our time back to the Lord, he promises that it will not be wasted.

TIRED

Who can help me when I grow weary?

He gives power to those who are tired and worn out; he offers strength to the weak. Even youths will become exhausted, and young men will give up. But those who wait on the LORD will find new strength. They will fly high on wings like eagles. They will run and not grow weary. They will walk and not faint. *ISAIAH 40:29-31*

The Sovereign LORD is my strength! He will make me as surefooted as a deer and bring me safely over the mountains. *HABAKKUK 3:19*

Fatigue makes us more vulnerable to temptation and danger. When we are weary, we should turn to the Lord for rest and refreshment. In his power, we will be able to go into every situation with a clear head and a steady hand.

Does my weariness disappoint God?

Each time he said, "My gracious favor is all you need. My power works best in your weakness." So now I am glad to boast about my weaknesses, so that the power of Christ may work through me. *2 CORINTHIANS 12:9*

Jesus said, "Come to me, all of you who are weary and carry heavy burdens, and I will give you rest." *MATTHEW 11:28*

Our weariness often makes us more aware of God's faithfulness.

TITHING

How does tithing affect my own finances?

"Should people cheat God? Yet you have cheated me! But you ask, 'What do you mean? When did we ever cheat you?' You have cheated me of the tithes and offerings due to me ... Bring all the tithes into the storehouse so there will be enough food in my Temple. If you do," says the LORD Almighty, "I will open the windows of heaven for you. I will pour out a blessing so great you won't have enough room to take it in! Try it! Let me prove it to you!" *MALACHI 3:8, 10*

God promises to meet our needs far and above our gifts to him. Tithing is God's means for supplying a variety of needs for his people. As we fulfill his command to meet others' needs, he graciously meets our own.

If you give, you will receive. Your gift will return to you in full measure, pressed down, shaken together to make room for more, and running over. Whatever measure you use in giving—large or small—it will be used to measure what is given back to you. *LUKE 6:38*

If we give, God has promised to give to us more than we can imagine! Those who trust this promise find that they always have what they need.

WILL OF GOD

Does God really have a plan for my life?

You chart the path ahead of me and tell me where to stop and rest. Every moment you know where I am. PSALM 139:3

The LORD says, "I will guide you along the best pathway for your life. I will advise you and watch over you." PSALM 32:8

The LORD will work out his plans for my life—for your faithful love, O LORD, endures forever. Don't abandon me, for you made me. PSALM 138:8

God has a plan for our lives. It is a journey with various destinations and appointments and a great deal of freedom as to the pace and scope of the travel. God's plan for us will always have a sense of mystery, but we can be certain that he will guide us as long as we rely on his leading.

How can I learn God's will for my life?

Seek his will in all you do, and he will direct your paths. PROVERBS 3:6

We can be confident that he will listen to us whenever we ask him for anything in line with his will. 1 JOHN 5:14

Prayer and the study of God's word are the most significant means that he uses to guide us.

Seek his will
in all you do,
and he will
DIRECT
your paths.

Proverbs 3:6

WISDOM

What are the benefits of wisdom?

Wisdom will multiply your days and add years to your life. If you become wise, you will be the one to benefit. If you scorn wisdom, you will be the one to suffer. *PROVERBS 9:11-12*

Trust in the LORD with all your heart; do not depend on your own understanding. Seek his will in all you do, and he will direct your paths. *PROVERBS 3:5-6*

A wise man is mightier than a strong man, and a man of knowledge is more powerful than a strong man. *PROVERBS 24:5*

How do we obtain wisdom?

If you need wisdom—if you want to know what God wants you to do—ask him, and he will gladly tell you. He will not resent your asking. *JAMES 1:5*

Let those who are wise listen to these proverbs and become even wiser. And let those who understand receive guidance by exploring the depth of meaning in these proverbs, parables, wise sayings, and riddles. Fear of the LORD is the beginning of knowledge. Only fools despise wisdom and discipline. *PROVERBS 1:5-7*

Come here and listen to me! I'll pour out the spirit of wisdom upon you and make you wise. *PROVERBS 1:23*

WITNESSING

How will God help me be a witness to my faith?

Jesus called out to them, "Come, be my disciples, and I will show you how to fish for people!" *MARK 1:17*

Sharing our faith is a natural expression of our fellowship with Jesus. As we pray for sensitivity to his leading, he promises to direct us to those who are ready to hear the Good News of salvation.

But what if I find it difficult to share my faith?

God has not given us a spirit of fear and timidity, but of power, love, and self-discipline. So you must never be ashamed to tell others about our Lord. And don't be ashamed of me, either, even though I'm in prison for Christ. With the strength God gives you, be ready to suffer with me for the proclamation of the Good News. It is God who saved us and chose us to live a holy life. He did this not because we deserved it, but because that was his plan long before the world began—to show his love and kindness to us through Christ Jesus. *2 TIMOTHY 1:7-9*

When the enemy tries to intimidate us with lies about our inadequacies, we can call upon the promise that the truth will set us free to share our faith boldly.

WORK

How is my work important to the Lord?

This should be your ambition: to live a quiet life, minding your own business and working with your hands, just as we commanded you before. As a result, people who are not Christians will respect the way you live, and you will not need to depend on others to meet your financial needs.
1 THESSALONIANS 4:11-12

If your gift is to encourage others, do it! If you have money, share it generously. If God has given you leadership ability, take the responsibility seriously. And if you have a gift for showing kindness to others, do it gladly. ROMANS 12:8

God blesses us when we do work that is in keeping with our gifts and abilities.

What does the Lord promise to those who work hard?

Good planning and hard work lead to prosperity. PROVERBS 21:5

Work hard and cheerfully at whatever you do, as though you were working for the Lord rather than for people. Remember that the Lord will give you an inheritance as your reward, and the Master you are serving is Christ. COLOSSIANS 3:23-24

God promises a reward to those who work hard. That reward can include financial prosperity. It may be the rewards of respect and personal satisfaction or the joy of contributing to the welfare of another.

WORRY

Where can I turn when worry overwhelms me?

So I tell you, don't worry about everyday life—whether you have enough food, drink, and clothes. Doesn't life consist of more than food and clothing? Look at the birds. They don't need to plant or harvest or put food in barns because your heavenly Father feeds them. And you are far more valuable to him than they are. Can all your worries add a single moment to your life? Of course not … So don't worry about tomorrow, for tomorrow will bring its own worries. Today's trouble is enough for today. *MATTHEW 6:25-27, 34*

What can I do with the problems that worry me?

Give your burdens to the LORD, and he will take care of you. He will not permit the godly to slip and fall. *PSALM 55:22*

Don't worry about anything; instead, pray about everything. Tell God what you need, and thank him for all he has done. *PHILIPPIANS 4:6*

Give all your worries and cares to God, for he cares about what happens to you. *1 PETER 5:7*

Prayer and a godly perspective drive worry from our minds and hearts. Peace comes when we pray, release all our cares to the Lord, and focus our minds on the promises of God.

INDEX